SEVONTI

META
MORPH
OSIS

Overcoming Adversity and
Unleashing the Best Version of You

emerge
publishing

25 24 23 22 21 20   8 7 6 5 4 3 2 1

METAMORPHOSIS — Overcoming Adversity and Unleashing the Best in You.
©2020 Sevonte Miller

TULSA, OKLAHOMA

Published by:
Emerge Publishing, LLC
9521B Riverside Parkway, Suite 243
Tulsa, Oklahoma 74137
Phone: 888.407.4447
www.EmergePublishing.com

Library of Congress Cataloging-in-Publication Data

ISBN: 978-1-949758-64-1 Paperback
ISBN: 978-1-949758-65-8 Digital/E-book

BISAC Category:
SEL044000   SELF-HELP / Self-Management / General
SEL023000   SELF-HELP / Personal Growth / Self-Esteem
EDU038000 EDUCATION / Student Life & Student Affairs

Printed in the United States.

TABLE OF CONTENTS

DEDICATION

To my beloved mother and grandmother, Yvonne Sunshine Miller and Lois Miller, who have instilled in me the value of having faith in God and know that he will always be there for you no matter what you may endure. My faith has become the foundation of my life and I have learned that without faith I wouldn't be where I am today.

To my father, Hosea Moseley, who has taught me the value of hard work. Your work ethic has never gone unnoticed. I thank you for instilling in me the value of hard work and the opportunities that it brings.

To my church family, who has been with me every step of the way. I thank you all for continuing to pray for me. I love you all dearly!

INTRODUCTION

Transformation Starts from Within

Metamorphosis: A term which means change, not just a change in physicality but also a change in mentality. As human beings we undergo a metamorphosis at a critical point in our lives. Without metamorphosis there can't be growth.

As children, we live life full of imagination and creativity. But then, something changes. We grow up and we lose that imagination and creativity in an effort to conform rather than stand out. We start to see the world as just black and white, not realizing that the colors of the rainbow still exist. We become stagnant, complacent, and idle, just living life on a day to day basis. Our passions, drive, and goals begin to disintegrate. In order for us to change and live not only a successful life, but also a fulfilling one, we must undergo a complete metamorphosis. Just as a caterpillar morphs into a butterfly, we must morph ourselves internally and externally in order for true change to take place. Without growth there can be no change and without change there can be no influence.

This book is dedicated not only to students in the academic field, but students of life who are struggling to find their way. It is for the individuals who not only feel like they want to give up and throw in the towel but also the ones who don't see a light at the end of the tunnel.

As both an undergraduate and a graduate student in college I had to face many trials and tribulations to achieve the level of success and comfort that I have within myself. I know what it's like to fail an exam, to drop a class, and to feel like a college degree isn't worth it. I know what it feels like to deal with depression, anxiety and having low self-esteem.

Many people don't know the efforts that I have taken to hide what I was going through. There are times when I didn't want to get up for class. I felt socially isolated and tried to fit in with various groups to fill the void, but I lost myself mentally, physically, and emotionally while doing so. Sometimes I felt as though a college degree wasn't worth the mental anguish I was facing. I was constantly being told by society that I was going to be in thousands of dollars of debt in student loans, that the degree I had wouldn't make me any money, or that college just wasn't for me. In this generation the suicide rates among college students is steadily increasing, and it is the second most common cause of death among college students.

You may be wondering what made me write this book about my own metamorphosis. My answer to that is you all, the readers. I always said as a child that someday I would make a change in this world. If I could make a positive impact on just one person's life I would be satisfied. I told myself that before I leave this Earth I don't want to be famous, I want to be effective. Fame is short-lived, but people will always remember the personal effect that you had in their life.

In this book, I talk about my metamorphosis throughout my personal and academic life. I talk about the various ups and downs that I have experienced and how I have been able to use each experience as an opportunity for growth. My goal is to be transparent enough so that you, the reader, will be able to use my experience for opportunities for growth as well.

I've realized two things in my short life thus far, the first of them being that we all are human. As humans we all have a variety of different personalities and emotions that are displayed. There are days when we are flooded with negative emotions even to the point of being suicidal. Then, there are days when we are bursting with positivity and happiness. The bottom line is that we are all human! I am telling you that it is okay to feel sadness, happiness and everything in between. We are each genetically, physically, emotionally, and mentally designed in our own special way, never forget that! No two people are exactly alike. Embrace that you are a unique and special individual and be confident in who you are and how you feel.

The second thing that I have realized in my 24 years is that as individuals we all have a choice. Life is a game of chess, in which we must make strategic choices every day to move forward and achieve the best possible outcome. When we wake up in the morning, we make the choice to stay in bed or to be productive. We choose whether we want to dominate the day or if we will allow the day to dominate us. This daily game of chess and the moves that we make manifest themselves as habits. These habits can have effects that are detrimental or beneficial in both our own lives and in the lives of others.

Our daily mindset provides the framework for our actions, which builds the foundation for our lives, which has the potential to propel us into our destiny. There is nothing as powerful as a changed mind. To alter the path of your destiny you must change the way that you view failures, mistakes, and frustrations. Success is the final destination, but the process is the journey. In all great adventure stories, the protagonist becomes the hero not only in spite of their trials, but because of them. You are the protagonist of your own adventure story! Throughout your journey you will experience depression, anxiety, and the burdens of life. You will discover who you truly are and what you are destined to do, becoming the hero of your story in the process. By discovering your self-worth, talents, and potential you undergo a process known as, "Self-Actualization."

By the end of this book you will learn how to shift your destiny from a person filled with frustration to a person filled with prosperity. To unleash your potential and take action in your life you have to undergo a metamorphosis not just physically, but mentally. You must first be knocked down in order to rise. My hope is that this book will inspire you to change your narrative from a story of defeat to one of a hero making a positive impact on this world.

With that being said, I ask that you walk with me through my own journey and learn how to stop limiting yourself and unleash your full potential.

Welcome to Metamorphosis.

—ɯɯ—

CHAPTER ONE

DEPRESSION: IN TOO DEEP

Depression is okay. In order for change to take place, you must first be crushed.

D epression: An umbrella term that can take on a variety of meanings. Depression can be temporary or it can be long-term. Depending on the individual. Depression among college students is steadily on the rise and doesn't appear to be decreasing any time soon. As college students we can become discouraged due to distressing grades, losing friendships, relationships, or feeling socially isolated.

The process of experiencing negative situations can be devastating in of itself, but to growth in life, we must be crushed. When you get crushed by the various tragedies in life, you are forced to reinvent and re-identify yourself in their wake. It's a process that has to take place and it can't be avoided. The focus, however, should not be on the hammer that is doing the crushing, or even the violent act itself. The focus should be placed on what there is to gain or learn by breaking the rock in the first place, the geode. Just as if we are too focused on the hammer we will not be able to see the crystals inside the rock, if we focus too much on the problem we will be unable to see the solution or the gain. The mentality that we take when facing an obstacle can mean the difference between being a simple crushed rock, or being a geode. It can mean the difference between being crushed by our destiny, or reaching it. We have to keep in mind that the problem is temporary, but it's our attitude towards the problem that will determine whether we overcome the issue or let the issue consume us.

"... Our outlook on life is a kind of paint brush and with it we paint our own world. It can be bright and filled with hope and satisfaction or it can be dark and gloomy. The world we experience is a reflection of our attitude."-Earl Nightingale

Our attitude determines our altitude.

College is known to be the best time of your life, where you are able to find yourself and realize who you truly are. My introduction into college was filled with obstacles that crushed me, and aided me on my journey to discover what type of geode I am and could be.

When I started college, I didn't know what to expect, and as the semester progressed I realized how socially isolated I had become. It essentially felt like I was starting my life over. I was without a local support system, work was beginning to pile up, and I was losing all of the motivation that I began with. I heard numerous of times that, "College is easy." I realized very quickly that, I had heard wrong. Every day I would go to class, go to the cafeteria, do homework and go to sleep. I didn't take advantage of the full freshman experience. My first semester I felt like I barely survived. I wasn't taking care of myself physically or mentally.

The second semester of freshman year life really hit me. I had a hard time trying to stay motivated and trying to see a light at the end of the tunnel. All I was seeing was complete darkness. I will never forget the class that changed my approach and perspective. It was a sociology class, 'Race, Class, Gender and Sexuality.' The first day of class the professor told us that her class was going to be challenging and that we would have to study to pass the class. At the time I was a pre-medical major and in my arrogance I didn't believe that the class was going to be a challenge because it was a social science class.

I specifically remember the first exam in the class which I barely prepared for, thinking that I didn't need to use too much effort. I procrastinated when it came to studying, constantly saying, "I'll just wait until tomorrow." This went on for days, which then turned into weeks. I stayed up all night studying the day before the exam and was drained the next day in class. Due to my lack of proper preparation I received a D on that first exam, and as a result I began the semester with a D in the class. I realized that every choice has a consequence.

I was able to attend college with a full ride in scholarships and didn't have to come out of pocket for tuition or housing. All I had to do was make good grades and stay out of trouble. I'd always been hard on myself when it came to my grades because I knew I had the potential to be great. That one grade made me realize that potential didn't matter if I didn't put it to use. I saw myself as a failure and fell into a pit of shame and depression. At that moment I wanted to give up and drop out of college. I didn't answer phone calls, I barely got out of bed, I missed some classes, and was overeating. I didn't talk to anyone or attend any school events. I felt like I had been crushed.

The first two weeks after I received a D on my exam I felt as though I wasn't good enough, and the thought of dropping out kept reoccurring. I kept telling myself, 'what's the point of continuing to go to college if you can't even pass an exam?' I felt hopeless.

I had to have a heart to heart conversation with not only myself but, God as well. I always told myself that, 'God gives his toughest battles to his strongest soldiers.' In that moment I had an epiphany. I realized that one exam grade would not determine my fate, if I wouldn't let it. I had to change my mindset and snap out of the depression I was in. I was greater than one bad exam.

I made up in my mind that I was going to do all that I could in order to get an A in the class. I went to my professor's office hours at least once a week and studied every single day to prepare for lecture and the upcoming exams. As a result, I made no less than an 88% on all of my exams for the rest of the semester and earned a final grade of a B+ in the class.

Even though I didn't achieve my goal of making an A in the class I still was proud of myself. I didn't let a temporary grade influence me to make a permanent decision about my college career. I kept pushing myself. I saw that B+ as motivation because I proved to myself that if I put my mind to a specific goal, self-manifestation will take place and everything will unfold right before my eyes. All I have to do is channel positive energy to that goal.

When I reflected on my freshman year, I can say that it was one of the best and one of the worse years of my college experience. Even though I was in a very deep depression, the perspective that I gained helped mold me into the person I am today.

There are times in life when failure hits, and it becomes easy to sink into depression. The most important thing to remember, however is that failure isn't permanent. We cannot be afraid to fail, as it is one of the many steps towards success. Beethoven was told by his music teacher that he was a hopeless composer but went on to become one of the greatest composers to ever live. Walt Disney was fired by the editor of a newspaper for lacking in ideas but went on to create his own empire. Oprah was told that she was unfit for television and was fired, but now she has a net worth of over $2 billion. Albert Einstein didn't speak until the age of four but came up with the Theory of Relativity. Bill Gates dropped out of Harvard and started Microsoft. Dr. Seuss' original manuscript was rejected 28 times and by the time of his death he had sold over 600 million copies of his book and it had been translated into 20 different languages. J.K. Rowling's book series Harry Potter was rejected numerous times and now she has sold over 450 million books worldwide. Steve Jobs dropped out of college after one semester and co-founded, 'Apple' and when he passed away his net worth was over $8 billion.

The one common factor that all successful people have in common is that they have all experienced failure at some point in their life. What separates the extraordinary from the ordinary is that they don't let their failures define them or limit them to what they can accomplish. Needless to say, negative thoughts will try to cloud your vision. The key is to have 'tunnel vision,' keep your eye on the prize, and know that failure is temporary. There are times when you're going to want to give up and throw in the towel, but just keep pushing yourself and focus on the light at the end of the tunnel.

—⚏—

Chapter Two

Anxiety: Will I Make It?

*Anxiety- An altered state of consciousness
that is pushing you to the next level.*

Anxiety is normal and is experienced by everyone. It's a behavior that correlates with feelings of embarrassment, rejection, loneliness, shame, frustration and confusion. Anxiety rises when you start to focus more on the future instead of worrying about what is happening in the present.

Anxiety is the hurricane of the mind. Your anxiety starts off as a tropical depression, barely noticeable. As your anxiety increases, it turns into a tropical storm. As time progresses and you continue to have reoccurring thoughts about your past or future, that tropical storm in your mind quickly develops into a hurricane. The anxious thoughts that you continue to have causes the outer bands of the storm to rise in intensity. Before you know it, the anxiety in your mind increased from a category one to a category five, thus causing utter mental destruction. Every hurricane has what is known as an 'eye.' The 'eye' is known as the region of the storm that is the most calm. The beauty is that we have the power to reduce the intensity of our mental hurricane by focusing our energy on the 'eye' of the storm, rather than the outer bands.

"You can't always control what goes on outside. But you can always control what goes on inside." -Wayne Dyer

At some point, you must ask yourself, *'Are my thoughts the master of me?'*

Or,

'Am I the master of my thoughts?'

You are in the driver seat of your life, and you set the pace. You are the only one who can determine what direction will take. When your anxiety is in the driver's seat, it's because you've succumbed to your thoughts, and you let them control you versus you controlling them.

As a college student you will experience anxiety throughout each semester, and sometimes it will be so severe that it will make you want to throw in the towel and give up. I've been in this situation, and I'm here to tell you that you just have to focus on what you can control.

After my trials during freshman year, I thought I had it all figured out for sophomore year, and once again, I was wrong. We always think that we have life figured out until it throws us a curve ball. There is a saying which states 'If you want to make God laugh, give him a fully developed plan of your life.' Clearly, I was the source of many laughs. At that time I was still a pre-medicine and psychology student. To qualify for medical school upon graduating, I had to pass organic chemistry one. After some hiccups, I had a successful freshman year and was looking forward to dominating sophomore year. As I was progressing through the semester I ended up having to withdraw from organic chemistry one because I did not pass any of the exams. At the end of the semester my anxiety had risen through the roof. I starting having re-occurring thoughts that I wasn't going to make it into medical school because I had a 'withdraw' on my transcript. Mentally I couldn't handle the class anymore and I decided to throw in the towel.

The following semester I decided to retake the class instead of allowing it to defeat me. The first day of class my anxiety was still high because I kept dwelling on the previous semester and how I performed in the class then. I was focusing more on the past than on the present and once again, I started to let my thoughts consume me.

In order to reduce my anxiety and pass the class I knew that I had to change my thought process. I realized that I didn't pass organic chemistry one the first time because I didn't set a goal for myself. I had no roadmap on how I was going to pass the class.

Orison Swett Marden stated it best, *"All who have accomplished great things have had a great aim, have fixed their gaze on a goal which was high, one which sometimes seemed impossible."*

Think of a planned and mapped out trip to Disneyland. You and your friends know exactly how long it will take to get there and where exactly it is in California. You all have a definite goal and it's a 9.9 out of 10 chance that you all will arrive at your destination.

Now let's say that you and your friends said that you all were going to just take a road trip. No roadmap and no final destination. Eventually you all will continue to drive until you can't drive anymore.

Needless to say, the more you start setting goals for yourself, the more likely you will achieve them.

As such, my ultimate goal for the semester was to pass my organic chemistry 1 class. In addition to that I set daily, weekly, and monthly goals in order to achieve the ultimate goal. I studied at least an hour each day for that class. I started grasping the concepts quicker, changed my thinking, and told myself that I could do it. I abandoned the pattern of thinking that I wasn't good enough to pass and adopted the thoughts that I was going to achieve my goal of passing the class. Needless to say, at the end of the semester I had successfully passed organic chemistry one.

I gave you this example to let you know that anxiety is nothing but an altered state of consciousness that shifts your perception to focusing more on the future than the present. Focus on what you can control right here and right now.

Cast all your anxiety on him because he cares for you.
1 Peter 5:7

Throughout the semester I constantly had to remind myself to have faith, not only in myself, but in God. Even when the road was tough I had to trust in Him to know that he wouldn't let me down. Prayer, faith and hard work and goal-setting is what helped me accomplish my goal of passing the class.

Always remember that all things that are worth it will take effort. As such, college will be tough, but the journey will be well worth it. When you start to feel anxious, take a deep breath, relax, regroup, work hard and continue to push yourself until you achieve your goal. And even if you don't achieve your goal be proud of yourself because you know that you gave it your all!

—⚭—

CHAPTER THREE

SELF ESTEEM:
WE ALL HAVE A STORY

To be of service to others, you must first help yourself.

Self-Esteem is an internal battle that people face it can be difficult to overcome.

In my childhood I was 5'2" and weighed 200 pounds.

When I met with my doctor he told me that I was obese and that if my weight continued to increase I would develop diabetes. I was placed on a strict diet for six months to gain control of my weight. As a result of the diet, my Body Mass Index (BMI) decreased significantly and I was in the correct range according to my age, weight and height. Even though I lost over sixty pounds I still felt like I was obese mentally, even though I wasn't physically. I walked around school with baggy clothes and wore a jacket constantly because I didn't want to be bullied for my weight.

I battled and continue to battle with low self-esteem. As the years progressed entering into my adolescent years I felt as if I was starting to gain confidence in myself only for it to be shot down by my peers. This struggle with self-esteem transitioned into my freshman year of college. I had gained what is known as the 'freshman 15.' That ended up turning into the 'freshman 40.' I walked to my lectures wearing oversized shirts and gym shorts because I couldn't fit any of my other clothes. At the time I wasn't taking care of myself mentally or physically and it showed by my appearance. I felt less than everyone else. Because my self-esteem was extremely low it caused me to become unmotivated to do anything.

As a college student you will have days where your self-esteem will be at an all-time low. But, you have to keep your head up and don't think that you are less than anyone. Self-esteem is nothing but a psychological mindset that traps you if you let it. Remember, you have the ultimate power.

There was an old saying, 'sticks and stones may break my bones, but words will never hurt me.' The truth is that words do hurt you. Words can hurt you more than sticks and stones. Words can destroy you mentally and emotionally. The goal is to replace these negative words with positive words.

I challenge you, for every negative thought that comes into your mind that tries to destroy your self-worth replace it with two positive thoughts.

Often times, we are our worst inner critic. We tell ourselves that we aren't good enough, we're not smart enough to pass that class, or we're too dumb to get a degree. All of these things are nothing but lies that we continuously put in our head which holds us back from achieving greatness. Our behaviors are a reflection of our thoughts. If you think that you are fat, then that thought can become a reality over time.

We all have different walks through life and to be of service to others, we must first help ourselves.

When we have low self-esteem and are constantly judging ourselves, we are more likely to project our own negative emotions and insecurities onto others. The saying goes, 'Hurt people, hurt people.' If we do not have the capacity to be kind to ourselves, how can we be capable of being kind to others? To empathize with our fellow humans and treat them with kindness in turn, we must first learn to be kind to ourselves.

"Empathy is about standing in someone else's shoes, feeling with his or her heart, seeing with his or her eyes. Not only is empathy hard to outsource and automate, but it makes the world a better place." –Daniel H. Pink

Life is tough and we constantly forget that not everyone's situation is the same. This is why we must practice empathy, as it is the foundation of friendships and relationships. As the years go by we tend to become bitter, our hearts change from warm and compassionate to cold and bitter. We start to develop this mentality that we constantly need to get ahead, and stay ahead of the next person. We don't have to help them, and if I can do it then they can do it too. This is not the case. As we get older we neglect the fact that, every person is not the same as you. They do not have the same DNA, nor were they born in the same environment that you were born in.

The truth of the matter is, you never know what someone is dealing with.

A prime example of this is how often times when we are driving and come to a red light, we may see a person who is homeless holding a sign on the side of the road and asking for anything to help. Most of us tend to act like we don't see them and keep looking forward. I am guilty of this as well. Many people have the same mindset of 'If I can be successful then they can too.'

The reality is that we are not showing compassion or empathy for the person. When is the last time that you asked a person experiencing homelessness what got them in the situation to becoming homeless, or when is the last time that they ate instead of judging them? These are thoughts that barely cross our minds because we are too judgmental and believe that most people who are homeless just want money for drugs and alcohol. In actuality we don't know what the person has been through. They could have just lost their job, spouse, family, we just don't know.

Practice empathy wherever you go because you have no way of knowing what the person had to go through to get to where they are. Just like when I made my first C in college which was in organic chemistry. A lot of people knew that I was intelligent when it came to my academics and that I took them very seriously. They were shocked when I announced that I made my first C grade. What they failed to realize was that I had withdrew from the class and had to retake it. There were plenty of nights that I broke down and started crying because I didn't think that I would pass.

I say all of this to say that empathy is the key to survival.

"In my view, the best of humanity is in our exercise of empathy and compassion. It's when we challenge ourselves to walk in the shoes of someone whose pain or plight might seem so different than yours that it's almost incomprehensible."- Sarah McBride

—◊◊◊—

CHAPTER FOUR

HUMILITY:
KILL YOUR PRIDE

To understand life we must understand who we are, to understand who we are, we must first gain humility.

Pride: An attitude that can lead quickly to self-destruction. With pride comes arrogance and an ego that is uncontrollable. As we go through life we can become prideful without realizing it and it only takes one event to humble us.

Criss Jami stated, *"Time and time again does the pride of man influence his very own fall. While denying it, one gradually starts to believe that he is the authority, or that he possesses great moral dominion over others, yet it is spiritually unwarranted.*

By that point he loses steam; in result, he falsely begins trying to prove that unwarranted dominion by seizing the role of a condemner."

I will never forget my freshman year of high school. At the time I was very involved in soccer and had been playing the sport since the age of six. I was very dedicated to the sport and played competitive soccer on the weekends and practiced during the weekdays. As high school season was approaching and tryouts began I had the dream that I was going to make the varsity team my freshman year. That dream did not come true and I accepted that and I was fine with playing on the junior varsity team. I had a very successful soccer season both in and outside of high school my freshman year.

Sophomore year had approached and soccer tryouts had begun. Something was different though. I had become full of myself and arrogant. I knew that I was going to be on the varsity team. I had met all of the qualifications that I needed to in order to be on the varsity team included running a half of mile in under three minutes. I had went around school telling my friends that I had made the varsity team and that I knew that I would make it because I thought I was one of the best players in the school. About a week went by and our coach compiled the results from tryouts and told us who made varsity and who made the junior varsity team. Most of my friends who I grew up playing soccer with made the varsity team and I didn't make the cut. I remember that day vividly. I didn't talk to anyone for a week because I was so disappointed in myself. I even went and asked my coach why I didn't make the team and he told me that I would barely get any playing time on varsity. I was going to quit playing all because I didn't make the varsity team, but my friends told me just to hang in there and that I would for sure make the varsity team the next year.

As time progressed during sophomore season I decided to play on junior varsity. The problem was that I still didn't learn my lesson on being prideful and arrogant and what it led to. During practice I slacked off and never gave it 100%. I joked around and talked back to the coaches because in my mind I was never wrong. I had the attitude that if I wasn't right then nobody was. It even had gotten to the point to where I was telling the coaches where to play me despite what they said.

It was a weekday game. I was playing outside defender. I was running and I suddenly collapsed to the ground. I was out the rest of the game. I could barely move. I had went to the doctors and they told me that I had torn my quad muscle and I pulled my hamstring all in the same season. I played at most, five games during my whole season sophomore year. Every time my quad and hamstring had gotten better I injured it all over again. But, looking back, this is what I needed. I needed to be humbled. My pride had gotten so strong that sooner or later it would have caused me to self-destruct.

As the season had come to an end I had to reflect not only over the season but over my life. I was so blessed yet so arrogant. I never knew where that pride came from but I knew that it had to be fixed and quickly. I knew that I had to change my ways.

During the off season I had completely recovered from my injuries and was in a better place mentally. Every morning and night I prayed asking God to humble me. The power of that one prayer changed my whole life. I no longer saw myself as the best one on the team, instead I saw myself as an equal. I became more of a team player and didn't argue with a teammate or coach.

Junior season tryouts had come around and I was in the best shape that I was ever in physically and mentally. I had trained twice a day, in the morning and in the evening. I went into tryouts with the mindset that I have to give it my all and the results will be based upon my efforts. When the final results were gathered, I was told that I made the varsity team. That was the best season in my high school career. I was unstoppable and I didn't let my pride get the best of me.

I mentioned this lesson in humility because sometimes we let our pride overstep boundaries that it should have never crossed in the first place.

"Pride is your greatest enemy,
humility is your greatest friend."
–John R. W. Stott

"Some never get started on their destiny because they cannot humble themselves to learn, grow, and change."
–Author Unknown

Pride is a problem that everyone will face over the course of their life. Our pride can hold us back from reaching our destiny. It can become a silent killer if we cannot detect it early. Once we are able to detect it then our lives begin to change. Once we start to transition from being prideful to becoming humble our lives begin to change drastically.

Always remember:

"Whoever exalts himself will be humbled, and he who humbles himself will be exalted." -Matthew 23:12

—w—

CHAPTER FIVE

COMMITMENT: 100% OR 0%, YOU DECIDE

Commitment is more than just a word,
it's a process that must be improved upon every day.

Commitment: it is one word with a powerful meaning. It's not just a word, but a pledge to dedicate yourself to something. Commitment is the driving force to achieving whatever you want or desire. With commitment you have to train your mind to believe that you will obtain what you want as long as you continue to work towards that goal every day. When you are completely focused on your goal laziness, procrastination and doubt will disappear and the only focus will be accomplishing that which you put your mind to. You will not be defeated if you are committed. You will only be defeated when you let the thought of defeat overtake your mind.

On the following page, there is a famous poem written by Jessie Belle Rittenhouse:

I Bargained with Life for a Penny

"I bargained with Life for a penny,
And Life would pay no more,
However I begged at evening
When I counted my scanty store;

For Life is just an employer,
He gives you what you ask,
But once you have set the wages,
Why, you must bear the task.

I worked for a menial's hire,
Only to learn, dismayed,
That any wage I had asked of Life,
Life would have paid."

–Jessie Belle Rittenhouse

I mention this poem because, as we get older we start to just go through the motions instead of trying to get the most out of life. We try to stay consistent yet we don't stay committed. We accept what life has given to us instead of taking what we want. If you ask for mediocrity then life will give you mediocrity. If you ask life for a penny then it will only give you a penny. But, the truth of the matter is you have to demand what you want out of life. The most critical lines are the last two, which say, "That any wage I had asked of Life, Life would have paid." Essentially, you decide what you want out of life. If you ask life for a million dollars, it already has given you the million dollars, you just have to work for it.

What does commitment mean?

Commitment is being dedicated.

In high school I learned the true lesson of being committed to a goal and giving it 100%.

Junior year of high school I failed what was known as the FCAT, which was a standardized test that I had to pass in order to graduate high school. I failed the reading segment of the test. Once I found out I failed I had to take remedial reading classes. I was laughed at because I didn't pass the exam. Some even laughed and said that I, 'couldn't read.' I had to take these classes for a year. Even though I was picked at I wasn't going to let that determine who I was or how smart I was.

I realized that I needed help and sought assistance because if I didn't pass this course then I wouldn't graduate high school, and then couldn't attend college. I registered with a learning center that provided the educational services I needed in order to pass the exam.

I committed myself 100% to achieving my goal of passing this standardized test to graduate from high school.

During my junior year I juggled soccer practice five days a week, classes every day, morning workouts and tutoring. Tutoring took place three days out of the week and even on the weekends. At the time my car had no air conditioning, and it was a long and hot ride. So I would work out in the morning, go to class, drive to tutoring and then go to soccer practice. This went on for a year. I was determined to do whatever it took in order to not only pass the FCAT but also to have a successful school year.

During that year I realized that commitment is key in whatever that you do. Don't just go through the motions, give it your all. This is exactly what I did. Needless to say at the end of the year I passed the reading portion of the standardized exam and I was able to graduate high school with my graduating class.

When I officially made my decision to go to Florida Atlantic University I knew that I had to be committed. I had earned enough money in scholarships to have all four years of my undergraduate degree paid for. But, I knew that throughout my four years I had to keep my eyes on the ultimate goal which was to graduate college. Being consistent isn't enough. It has to be combined with commitment.

Whatever you have to do in life whether in or out of college make sure that you give it you're all. If you are only going to give 25% or 50 % of commitment then you might as well stop because you are wasting your time. You are merely going through the motions.

Commitment is a choice. You have to make up in your mind whether you are going to give it 100% or 0%. When you are truly committed, excuses don't exist. Despite all the odds that might be against you, being committed will keep you focused.

"Most people fail not because of a lack of desire but because of a lack of commitment" –Vince Lombardi

—〰—

CHAPTER SIX

INFLUENCE: DON'T BE FAMOUS, BE EFFECTIVE

The goal is not to be famous but be effective, influence first the individual, then true change will take place.

We live in a time where people are becoming famous but not being effective.

What does it mean to be effective?

Being effective means making a change not only in your life, but in the lives of others. You don't have to be famous to be effective. Just make up in your mind that you want to change your community, your country, or the world and just go out and do it. Do not limit yourself on what you can accomplish and never limit your point of entry! If you have an idea on how you want to change the world and it doesn't work out one way find other ways that will work. Just like if you lock yourself out of the house. There is more than one way to get inside, if you can't go through the front door or the back door then go through the window. Never say that you can't do something. When you limit yourself on what you can accomplish you are putting yourself into a mental prison and giving yourself a life sentence. Once you start limiting yourself your goals, dreams, and passions will not manifest because you have mentally imprisoned them. The power of our thoughts can be life changing.

Some of the greatest leaders like Mahatma Gandhi, Martin Luther King Jr., and Nelson Mandela all decided that they wanted to make an impact on this world for the better. They didn't care about being famous, they just wanted to be of service and help people. Mahatma Gandhi became known for leading nonviolent protest, Nelson Mandela became known for fighting for the freedom of his people, and Martin Luther King Jr. was known as one of the greatest civil rights leaders in the United States of America fighting for equal rights. I always told myself that I want to make a difference in this world but I didn't know how I was going to do it I just knew that I would.

"You must be the change you wish to see in the world."-
Gandhi

"Influence is when you are not the one talking and yet your
words fill the room; when you are absent and yet your presence
is felt everywhere." – TemitOpe Ibrahim

As a graduate student I constantly told myself that I wanted to help others, in particular college students all around the world. It was merely a dream that eventually turned into a reality. As I continued to engage in conversations with college students I heard them say that they were depressed, anxious, burnt out, about to have a mental break down, and other things that aren't discussed enough. I noticed that college students needed more help and that they might not be comfortable talking to someone about their problems. This is why I started my podcast, *#DearCollegeStudents*.

I started *#DearCollegeStudents* on April 16, 2019. I wanted to be of service to college students who truly needed help and guidance. When I first started my podcast I only had five plays within the first week. I truly thought that my podcast wasn't going to be successful and it wasn't going to be heard by people who needed to hear it. I started to have these thoughts that I had failed myself and that me making the podcast wouldn't help anyone.

"An inheritance gained hastily at the beginning will not be blessed at the end."-Proverbs 20:21

God's timing is everything. I had to realize that my timing did not matter.

I continued to produce more content despite my discouragement, and went from five plays in April to two thousand plays in October. Since October my podcast has expanded to eight different platforms with viewers in over 60 countries around the world.

I have set my mind to being effective and I will not stop until I am able to reach every college student around the world. I had to realize that I was the only one stopping myself from reaching millions of college students. In the beginning I wasn't as consistent as I could have been. When I shifted my mindset to thinking more positively about my podcast and how it was helping others I noticed that my audience increased drastically.

Dreams are nothing but dreams until they are put into action. Whatever dreams you have, you need to put them into action. Don't focus strictly on the results, but the journey, and everything will fall into line. That may be becoming a business owner or the president of your country, but do not give up on your dreams. The only person that stands in the way of you accomplishing your dreams is you. It all starts in the mind.

You have to have enough faith to know that you are going to accomplish and receive everything that you want out of life. Even if the results aren't showing the efforts that you are putting in, do not become discouraged.

Before Colonel Sanders became known as the creator of Kentucky Fried Chicken, he had his recipe turned down 1,009 times before being accepted once. But that one acceptance changed his entire life. He started at the age of 65 and became known globally as the creator of Kentucky Fried Chicken.

I mention Colonel Sanders story to inspire you to continue to think big, dream big, and never give up on your dream no matter what age you are or your circumstances.

Change your mindset and it will change your situation.

James Allen stated it like this:

"ALL THAT a man achieves and all that he fails to achieve is the direct result of his own thoughts."

It always starts with you.

CHAPTER SEVEN

GRIT:
FIGHT THROUGH

Grit is more than just strength of character, it's about giving your all, having faith, and leaving it all on the table.

On May 10, 2018, I received a letter in the mail saying that I was accepted into the Master of Science in Neuroscience program at Morehouse School of Medicine. I was ecstatic and I remember that I had always wanted to attend school at Morehouse. I scheduled a trip to tour the school and it was amazing. I had my eyes set on attending. On the way back from Atlanta, Georgia I remember sitting on the plane questioning if I really wanted to attend school there. I contemplated the entire flight back home. Even though I loved the school my passion wasn't in Neuroscience.

On April 12, 2018, a month prior to my acceptance to Morehouse I was accepted into the Master of Social Work program at Florida Atlantic University.

As soon as I graduated I had to make a decision about which program I wanted to earn my Master's degree in. I gave up my chance to attend my dream school and I ultimately chose to earn my Master's degree in Social Work at Florida Atlantic University. That was the best decision that I have ever made.

People have asked me:

"Why Social Work?"

"Why did you choose that profession?"

I have also heard:

"You will never make any money as a Social Worker."

"You will have to work two jobs in order to make ends meet."

Richard P. Feynman said it best, *"You have no responsibility to live up to what other people think you ought to accomplish.*

I have no responsibility to be like they expect me to be. It's their mistake, not my failing."

Earl Nightingale went on to say:

"Don't concern yourself with the money. Be of service ... build ...work ...dream ...create! Do this and you'll find there is no limit to the prosperity and abundance that will come to you."

What people fail to realize is that money comes and goes, you can be rich and miserable or poor and happy.

I knew what God called me to do and that was to be of service to other people and I knew that everything else would fall in line.

I had to constantly tell myself that, "A Lion doesn't concern himself with the opinions of the Sheep," they are on two different levels. People didn't understand why I chose the path that I chose because they couldn't relate to me, we had two different mindsets.

"Understanding is deeper than knowledge. There are many people who know you, but there are very few who understand you."-Author Unknown

August 21, 2018 was the first day of graduate school. I remember sitting in class and not knowing what to expect.

Thoughts continuously raced through my mind about if I had made the right decision. After the first week of classes I knew that I made the right decision. I loved the social work program, the professors, and my cohorts. I chose social work because I realized that it was my passion. The program continues to bring out the best in me. I learned quickly that in the program that you can't save everyone but sometimes it is the one person or family that you did save that will make up for the other 10 or 15 that you couldn't save.

But needless to say, every graduate program has its challenges. I had mental milestones that I had to overcome to be successful in the program. Graduate school is tough and it will challenge you but it makes you stronger mentally. There were days that I felt unmotivated to do anything. Sometimes you will experience burnout or even compassion fatigue. During my first year of graduate school I was making excellent grades but I wasn't taking care of myself physically. It was becoming difficult for me to get out of bed and to complete my class work. There were days when I just sat in my room stressing about how I was going to complete this paper or prepare for that exam. I was starting to isolate myself and complain about everything pertaining to school. I felt as if I was going through my freshman year of college all over again. I realized this and had to correct my behavior.

I had to do some self-reflecting and remember why I was in graduate school in the first place. I had to remember that everything was going to work out for my good. I had to continue to have faith, work hard, be committed, and be consistent. Faith was the foundation and still is the foundation of my life.

Grit plays a key role for me in graduate school. Grit is fueled by passion, motivation, and the will to never give up no matter what. I realized that I had endured so much in the past that I couldn't let anything hold me back from reaching my goal. If you would have asked me in the past if I saw college as an option I would have just laughed. My grandma, who I was very close with, passed away when I was in middle school. My mom and I were in over $200,000 worth of debt, and if I wanted to go to college she told me that I had to work hard for it because she couldn't afford it.

I say this to say that nothing is impossible.

Nelson Mandela stated:

"It always seems impossible until it's done."

Whenever you see the word, 'Impossible' break it into two words, 'I'm Possible.' Never think that you are no less than anyone else. Never think that you are better than anyone else.

Never compare yourself to anyone else. And always remember that where you are right now is right where you need to be and that timing is everything.

As I close this chapter I want you to always remember to keep fighting. You will have your good days and your bad ones. You will have sunshine and you will have rain. You will endure heartache and pain. You will experience adversity and defeat. You will not win every battle that you face. But never give up. Never throw in the towel. You are one step away from stepping into your purpose. Continue to believe in yourself, even when no one else believes in you. Be your own biggest cheerleader. Motivate yourself so that you can motivate and influence others. Be kind. Be empathetic. Be a crutch to whoever needs it. Life is about building each other up and bringing out the best not only in yourself but in others.

Steve Jobs stated it best:

"Your work is going to fill a large part of your life, and the only way to be truly satisfied is to do what you believe is great work. And the only way to do great work is to love what you do. If you haven't found it yet, keep looking. Don't settle. As with all matters of the heart, you'll know when you find it."

And always remember, never dwell in frustration, for it is not permanent, but be joyful in prosperity, embrace it, for it is a moment that leads into new beginnings.

A NOTE TO THE READER:

HOW DO YOU WANT
TO BE REMEMBERED?

E very second that passes with life is a second closer to death. Two dates will appear on the tombstone, the day that we are born and the day that we die. The problem arises when we focus too much on death and not enough on life. Life is precious, enjoy it. Ask yourself, 'Are you alive, or are you just living?'

The clock of life ticks continuously and before we know it, we will be lying on our death bed reminiscing about the, could've, should've, and would've.

Today is the day to ask yourself:

"How do I want to be remembered?"

This is the question that has resonated with me since October 2, 2019. As I sit in bed reflecting on this question, I've realized what's most important in life. In this age our world is consumed by glamour, fame, and the need to be validated. Too much social media, not enough human interaction. Too much complaining, not enough satisfaction. Cell phones are ruining friendships and relationships. Arrogance is replacing humility. Jealousy is replacing kindness. Morals are becoming non-existent. Instead of building one another up, we continue to tear each other down.

I asked myself, *'How do I want to be remembered?'*

I was born on September 29, 1995 and I am 24 years old at the time of this writing. Though I am still young I have endured adversity. We as humans cannot control the environment that we grew up in, but we can control whether or not we become a product of our environment. I want you all to remember that it is your mind that you must first change. Learn to be content, but not complacent. You will have good and bad days. But, you must see it through. Rise up and face obstacles head on, set goals out of this world and work until you accomplish those goals.

Unleash your full potential, don't just go through the motions. Instead of just using 10% of your potential, use 110%.

I want to be remembered as a person who made a positive impact in this world. I always told myself that I could care less about being rich and famous, I just want to be effective. Before I leave this Earth I want to give faith to the faithless, hope to the hopeless, and let anyone know who is reading this book that they can make it.

Now, *'How would you like to be remembered?'*

*Do you want to be remembered as a fighter
or a person who gave in?*

*A person who made a change in the world
or conformed to it?*

A person who chased their passion or let it wither away?

A person who set limits or broke limits?

A person who overcame adversity or succumbed to it?

A prisoner of your mind or a conqueror of it?

Always remember, the power lies within you.

—⁂—

About the Author

Sevonte Miller is a graduate of Florida Atlantic University. He received his Bachelors of Arts degree in Psychology at Florida Atlantic University and currently working on his Master's degree in Social Work at Florida Atlantic University. He started his own podcast called, '#DearCollegeStudents.' This podcast was created in order to help and motivate students to push through college. Through this podcast his goal is to inspire and let students know that they can make it through college no matter what circumstances or situations that may come up in their lives, all they have to do is continue to work hard and have faith in themselves and know that college is temporary and not their final destination.